Some Lessons Learned In Life

Synthia Zarreen

BookLeaf Publishing

India | USA | UK

Presentation by *BookLeaf Publishing*

Web: www.bookleafpub.com

E-mail: info@bookleafpub.com

ISBN: 9789357214773

First edition 2022

To all the people who love to read,

Learn, grow & be the best they can be.

ACKNOWLEDGEMENT

Thank you to all the people who support me and love me just the way I am.

Thank you to all the people who opposed me and tried their level best to destroy my confidence in myself, who tried to manipulate me and ruin my authentic self.
At the end of all their silly attempts, they only benefited me to strengthened my confidence in myself, be more courageous and truly be who I am meant to be.

PREFACE

In life we all go through ups and downs.
There are some painful moments, some pleasant moments.

After going through all those moments, when we reflect within, we realise the lessons those moments were trying to give to us.

Once we accept the lesson and let go of the painful experiences, we recall our past, our experiences without pain.

My book is about some of my observations of my experiences and the lessons that I learned. These lessons stayed with me as I journey through my life. They benefited me to build my strength, my courage, my confidence.

I hope in some way they benefit those who read my writing.

I Know I Exist

I know I exist.
Whether you accept me
Or reject me,
I do not need the permission
Of another human being
To know I exist.
Since I exist I matter.

I know I exist.
My energy exist,
With this body
Without this body
My existence is
Not dependent on this body.
My existence is
Simply being the energy
I am designed to be.

I know I exist.
My love exists.
Whether you love me
Or you hate me
My love exists.
My love does not depend
On your love to exist.

My love exists
Because I am capable
Of giving love to others
Irrespective of
Who they choose to be.

I know I exist.
My life exists,
Whether you understand my life
Or you do not understand my life
My life is
Not dependent on
Your opinion
Of what you think
Of my life.

I know I exist.
My worth exist,
Whether you realize
My worth
Or you do not realize
My worth,
I know
I am worthy.

I know I exist.
My happiness exist.
Whether you are happy
To know that I am happy

Or you fail to be happy
To know that I am happy
I know I exist
In a state of true happiness.

Dangerous

I am more dangerous
Than a dragon,
You know why,
Because I am human being
Who is wise.

Because I am someone
Who has nothing
To prove to anyone.

Because I am someone
Who knows I am worthy.
I am worthy of
All the good that
Life can offer.

I am more dangerous
Than a dragon,
You know why,
Because dragon is not real
But I am.

I am more dangerous
Than a dragon,
You know why,

My carelessly spoken words
Can hurt a person,
My indifference can
Cause pain in a heart that loves.
My absence can
Ruin someone's happiness.

I am more dangerous
Than a dragon,
You know why,
Because I don't look dangerous
But I am dangerous.

I am more dangerous
Than a dragon,
So beware all those people
Who oppose me,
Who move towards me
With the will to break me,
Who move towards me
With the intention of stopping
My free spirit from flowing,
The power of my good will
Can break your ill will into pieces.

I am more dangerous
Than a dragon,
So this is my advice to you.
Please handle me with care.

Those who do not know
How to handle a person
With love, care and kindness
Please stay away from me.

I am more dangerous
Than a dragon,
So if you get hurt
When you tried to manipulate me,
Please do not tell me
I did not warn you.

Overcoming Grief

When you go through grief,
You grief for a long time.
And than one day
Someone within you scream,
Enough is enough
No more grief,
No more living being sad.

You reject being consumed by grief.
The strength and courage to live
Wakes up within you.
You start feeling stronger,
You start to separate yourself
From that grief and move out
Of that state of grief.

You do not allow grief
To consume any part of your life.
You learn to live your life
After experiencing grief
Without losing your capacity
To be happy.

You learn to accept
The absence of the physical presence

Of the loved one.
You learn to live
With an empty space in your life.
You learn not to be bothered
By any form of emptiness ever again.

Slowly slowly you heal
And rebuild your world.
You accept the fact that
There is an empty space
In your world.

You will be you again,
But the new you
Will be much more brave,
Stronger and wiser
As you have experienced true grief
And overcame that grief.

Loneliness

Do you know
When you actually feel lonely?

You actually feel lonely
When you are surrounded
By people you thought
Would understand you,

And than you realise
They are all living
In their own world
Too scared to love,
Too scared to connect.

They have no clue
What is happening to you.
They cannot understand you,

They see you
But they do not notice you,

They can hear you
But they do not listen to you.

They fail to connect with you,

They fail to maintain
Good relationship with you.

It feels like
People, people everywhere
Not enough space
For you to stand,

People, people everywhere
Not a single one
Really willing to understand.

Universe With You

Do not feel lonely,
The entire universe
Is connected to you,
Is with you,
Supporting you.

The energy of the universe
Works in harmony
With your energy.

There is a flow of energy,
There is communication
Between you and the universe.
You are never alone.

As long as
You are not resisting,
There is an invisible energy
Supporting you.

Listen to the frequency,
You can feel it.
You can understand the language.

There is a message for you

In the Universe
Accept that message.

Never Lonely

Only when you expect
To be part of a group
But you are not in a group,

When you expect
To be part of a crowd,
But you don't fit into the crowd
You feel alone and lonely.

When you don't have
Any expectations
From any person,
From any group,
From any crowd,
You are never lonely.

You enjoy doing your own thing.
You enjoy being in your own space.
You enjoy your own companionship.

When you choose solitude,
You feel calm,
You are never alone.
You are your true friend.

Once you understand
The beauty of being on your own,
You would prefer people
Leave you alone and
Not bother you when they fail
To understand you.

Be someone
Who is not scared
To be on their own.
When you are tired
Rest for a while,

When you want to
Understand yourself better,
Reflect inwards.

Do not look for validation from others.
Look inside yourself and understand
Your strengths and weaknesses.

Work to reduce your weaknesses,
Do things that reinforces your strengths,

Know yourself.
Than the lies others tell you
Would not bother you.
You will never feel lonely.

I am a lover who declares war

I am a lover,
Who declares war
To protect those I love,
From those who
Try to hurt
My loved ones.

I declare war
Only because
I truly love.

Only to express
My true love
For my loved ones
I go into war
Against those who
Try to hurt
My loved ones.

This war is
Only an expression
Of my true love.

I am a lover
Who declares war.

Who you are

When your heart
Do not understand
Who you are,

And believes the lies
Others tell you
Regarding yourself,

You feel restless,
You feel confused,

You are uncertain,
You are angry,
You are frustrated.

You feel like
You do not know yourself.
You do not know
What to believe,
Who you are meant to be.

When you finally
Reflect inward
To know yourself,

You discover your truth,
Accept your truth,
And your heart start
Understanding your true self.

You understand what
You are meant to do
You find your purpose.
You heart feels calm,

All the lies you heard
Others say about you
Move away from you.

Your existence returns
Back to innocence and
Your true beauty shines.
You transform and
Embrace your true self.

You complete the work and
Fulfill your purpose.
You become
Who you are meant to be.
Your true authentic self.

Forgive yourself and your parents

Forgive your parents
For not understanding you,
When you desperately wanted them
To understand you.

Forgive your parents
For all the time
They were angry with someone else,
But mistreated you
In their state of anger.

Forgive your parents
For all the time
Instead of reflecting inwards
And reduce their weaknesses,
They pointed out your weaknesses
And made you think
You are not good enough.

Forgive your parents
For all the time
You wanted them to stand with you,
And say they loved you,
And show they cared for you,

But your parents went against you
And pointed fingers at you
Together with the world.

Forgive your parents
When they convinced you
That you are not worthy of love
Just the way you were.

Forgive your parents
For all the time they failed
To love you unconditionally,
And they demanded
You love them unconditionally.

Forgive your parents
For all the time
They insisted you ruin your happiness.
To make them happy.

Forgive your parents
For all the times
They claimed to love you.
When all you felt was emptiness,
And emotionally unavailable adults
Doing what they thought
Was expected of parents
To do in their society.

And also forgive yourself
For all the time
You didn't unconditionally love yourself,
And expected others
To love you unconditionally.

Forgive your parents,
And forgive yourself.
Just understand this
We are all doing the best
We can do with our
Limited knowledge,
Limited understanding.

We are just being human.
Doing the best we can do
At that moment.

Forgiveness

I forgive myself
For all of the times
I hurt myself.

I forgive myself
When I ignored
My own needs,
Lowered my standards
To accommodate someone
In my world.

I forgive myself
For all the pain
I willingly gone through,
So that the people
I loved would get
What they demanded
From me.

I forgive myself
For all the times
When I felt ashamed
To be my authentic self.

And I forgive myself

For all the time
I suffered in silence,
And I did not walk away
From an abusive relationship.

And I forgive myself
For all time
I wasted my time and energy
To fight battles
That were not mine to fight.

And I forgive myself
For all the time
I failed to give myself
The love I had every right
To give to myself.

I forgive myself
And for all the times
I believed the lies
Other told me about myself.

Now that I forgive myself,
I embrace my authentic self,
I embrace who I am truly.

Now that I forgive myself,
And I believe in myself,

I know I am not broken,
I live in a state of abundance,
I know I am a beautiful human being.
I believe I am enough just the way I am.

Now that I forgive myself,
I am starting to notice my strength,
I am realizing my worth,
I am recognising my own beauty.

Healing

Healing starts with
Understanding and accepting
The fact that you are in pain.

Healing begins with
Rejecting all lies
You tell yourself
To cope with the pain.

You need to do
Lot of self analysis
And understand
How to untangle
Yourself from that pain.

You need to
Attend to your wound,
Take care of yourself,
Be kind to yourself.

Hurting others has nothing
To do with healing.
But yes staying away
From those who
Wounded you in the first place

Is a good idea,
At times necessary
To protect your well-being.

Spiritual awakening

After a spiritual awakening,
You start living in harmony
With yourself,
With the Universe.

You don't try to
Fit into the crowd anymore.

This Universe is big enough
For all of us
Just the way we are.

After spiritual awakening,
You just give others around you
Space and time
To adjust to your presence,

To accommodate
Their version of you
Into their world.

Some invents a version of you
That's close to your reality,

Some invents a version of you

That's far from your reality.

Whatever they think of you
They think from their
Level of understanding.

Their idea about you
Is a reflection of
Their level of intelligence
And has nothing to do with
Your actual reality.

After a spiritual awakening
You have nothing
To prove to anyone.
You live in your space,
And you let others
Live in their space.

Darkness

Darkness is absence of light.
In state of darkness,
The meaning and
Value of light becomes clear.

Light and Darkness exist within
This Universe so that
The true meaning of each word,
Value and importance
Of each becomes clear.

For human beings to grasp
The meaning of light,
The importance of light,
There is a need for darkness
To exist in this Universe.

Now we as humans,
After understanding
Darkness and Light,
Have to make a conscious choice,
Which aspect to develop within us

Whether to nurture
The light within us

Or the darkness within us.

When you choose to nurture
the Light within you.
Darkness leaves you.

When you choose to nurture
The darkness within you
The darkness outside consumes you
Fills the spaces within you.

Choose wisely for
What choices you make
You live with the consequences
For making that choice.

We all have our baggage of darkness.
We need to handle and sort
Unwanted experiences and feelings.

Each person knows what darkness
Each have overcame
To fully embrace their light,
The journey is not always easy.

But I always believe
The human spirit is stronger
Than any darkness,

You are stronger than
Any baggage of darkness
You have to sort
In your life.

Never underestimate
The courage of your human spirit,
Recognise the strength of your will,
You are a human being for a reason .

Darkness can try to consume you
Let your light eliminate all the darkness
That tries to come near you.

Don't be scared of darkness
Let your light be so strong,
That in your presence
Darkness vanishes.

Let your light be so intense
That darkness moves away from you.

As more and more light
Grows within you,
The darkness moves
Further and further
Away from you.

What is normal?

What is normal?

Each society have
Their own definition of normal.

And each human being have
Their own definition of normal.

As society and human being
In the society is developing,
The definition of normal
Is changing and transforming.

There is no fixed
Definition of normal.
You choose what
Feels normal to you.

Consult with your heart
If doing something
Makes sense to you,
Makes your heart happy
And you are not ashamed
Of doing that,
Just do it.

Be so disciplined within,
You are always free to do
What you truly desire to do.

Love yourself

When you are sincerely
A giving person,

There are lot of people
Who doesn't care.
And they will drain you
If you are not consciously
taking care of yourself.

We, those who are
Caring and giving
Should time to time
Remind ourself,
That giving yourself should
Also be a priority,
Taking a break,
Resting is also required.

We are only a human being
Working utilising a body
With limitations,
Mind that becomes tired,
Heart that is capable of getting hurt.

In this realm of existence,

Taking care of yourself
Should be a priority.

From time to time
Take a break from
The noise of the world.
Feel the rhythm of your heart,
Feel how your heart
Happily dance to be alive.

Life

Life is a combination
Of painful and pleasant experiences.

All of our experiences
Gives us a beneficial lesson
That supports us to move on
To the next phase of our life.

Once you accept your life
Just the way your life is
You are not bothered
By the pain.
You don't get distracted
By the pleasure.

You simply enjoy your life
Without being consumed by life.

You rule over your life.
You are in charge of your life.
You choose whether
You are happy or sad
With whatever you have
experienced in your life.
You form your own perception.

Memories of this life
Lives within your soul,
Enrich your soul forever.

This is the first and last time
You are visiting this place.
This is your life.
Be the best you can be.

Death

The thought of death
Is not scary,
You are taught lesson
About death
From the moment
You and this world meet.

One day you are born
And one certain fact
About human being is
One day you will be gone.

So as long as you live,
Live fully,
Live properly,
Live wisely.

Pray for those
Who have already departed.
Value those who are
Your companion in this world.

Build beautiful memories
With your loved ones.

For one day
They will be gone.

Fight only for right reason,
Give love, receive love.
Be alive every season.

Enjoy your precious time
Live a good life every day
Taste death in a good way.

Mistakes

This is the beauty of
being a human,

You can make a mistake
Still learn something of value.

Once you recognise that
You did something wrong
You notice the lessons
That you are meant to learn
That can benefit you
In the long run.

Don't be afraid of
Making a mistakes.
Take responsibility,
Don't lie to yourself that
You don't make mistakes.

Life is perfect
With all the imperfections.
This is how life is meant to be.

Live, love, laugh & learn.
From what you see and don't see.

Enjoy being human
As best as you can be.

Meaningful work

It's a blessing to have
Meaningful work
In this world.

Be in love with life.
Life won't disappoint you.
Mostly people disappoint us
But we get angry with our life.

Life is precious,
Life is beautiful.
Take care of yourself,
Be your own best friend.

Eat what you love,
Wear something you love,
Do what makes you happy.

If possible go to different places.
Explore beautiful spaces.
Where you can breathe clean air,
Where you can feel energetic,
Where you can feel alive.

You are important

In your own world.
Rest to recharge yourself.
Work and rest,
Be your best.

Observe & Witness

When you can observe
As a witness
What is happening
In your life,

You can separate yourself
From what is happening
In your life.

You can enjoy your life
Without being consumed
By your life.

Losing and gaining,
Giving and receiving,
Are just some experiences
You can learn from.

You do not get overwhelmed
By the different experiences
You witness
On this Earth.

You are more than
Your experiences and

The lessons learned
From those experiences.

You are more worthy
And valuable than
The life you are living.

Wise & Fools

For the wise
This world is filled
With pure magic

For the fools
This world is filled
With events that
They label as tragic.

For the wise
There are lessons
To be learned
Respect to be earned.

For the fools
Their life is
Full of pain
Living life
Without anything
Meaningful to gain.

For the wise
Life is about
Expanding
Their consciousness.

For the fools
Life is all about
Winning and losing
Which after a point
Becomes pointless.

For the wise
Is the way to enlightenment
Which lasts forever.

For the fools
Is the way to entertainment
Which last until death is sent.

www.ingramcontent.com/pod-product-compliance
Lightning Source LLC
LaVergne TN
LVHW021254200726

843509LV00012B/1662